THE *Frank Loesser* SONGBOOK

ISBN 0-7935-2181-5

A Publication of

 FRANK MUSIC CORP.

EXCLUSIVELY DISTRIBUTED BY

 **HAL•LEONARD™ CORPORATION**

7777 W. BLUEMOUND RD. P.O. BOX 13819 MILWAUKEE, WI 53213

*Frank Loesser and Abe Burrows all smiles after winning the Pulitzer Prize for **How To Succeed in Business Without Really Trying** in 1962.*

THE *Frank Loesser* SONGBOOK

CONTENTS

#31852225   MUS.
S-9200   M784.5
L826

Loesser Family: John Loesser, Hannah Loesser, Frank Loesser, Jo Loesser and Susan Loesser at home on East 70th Street in 1962. Photo by Sam Shaw

Frank Loesser receiving an award from President Truman for "Rodger Young."

*t. Frank Loesser and Arthur Schwartz in 1943 after writing the score for **Thank Your ▪cky Stars**, an all-star movie written to raise money for U.S. War Bonds.*

Frank Loesser and his buddy George Raft in 1941.

◀ Silvers, Carl Reiner, Groucho Marx, Edward G. Robinson, Harry Ruby, Frank Loesser and Rex Harrison at a Hollywood party in 1941.

*Still from **Red, Hot and Blue**, Betty Hutton film for which Frank wrote the songs and made only film appearance as a piano-playing gangster.*

rank Loesser has been called the most versatile of all Broadway composers. His five musicals, WHERE'S CHARLEY?, GUYS AND DOLLS, THE MOST HAPPY FELLA, GREENWILLOW, and HOW TO SUCCEED IN BUSINESS WITHOUT REALLY TRYING, each a unique contribution to the art of American musical theater, were as different from each other as they were from the theater of their day. By the time WHERE'S CHARLEY? was produced in 1948 he was an established Hollywood songwriter with such enormous popular hits to his credit as "Spring Will Be A Little Late This Year" and "On a Slow Boat to China" (words and music); "The Boys In The Back Room" with Frederick Hollander; "I Don't Want to Walk Without You" with Jule Styne; "Two Sleepy People" and "Heart And Soul" with Hoagy Carmichael; "They're Either Too Young or Too Old" with Arthur Schwartz and "The Lady's In Love With You" with Burton Lane. He capped these successes in 1949 by winning the Academy Award on his own for "Baby, It's Cold Outside."

Born June 29, 1910, in New York City, Frank never studied music formally, although he couldn't help coming under its influence in his childhood. His father was a distinguished German-born teacher of classical piano and his older brother, Arthur, was a renowned concert pianist, musicologist, and music critic. He wrote his first song at the age of six ("The May Party"), but Frank refused to study classical music. His interest was in pop music, which his father disdained. So he taught himself, first the harmonica, then the piano in his early teens. He attended Townsend Harris High School and the City College of New York, but dropped out during the Depression and supported himself with an array of jobs that included selling newspaper advertising, working as a process server, and his favorite, City Editor of a short-lived newspaper in New Rochelle, NY.

Intrigued by word play, Frank began to write songs, sketches and radio scripts. He teamed up with William Schuman, who later became a serious composer and President of the Juilliard School. In 1931, they wrote "In Love With A Memory of You," Frank's first published lyric. Of this Schuman later said, "Frank Loesser has written hits with Hoagy Carmichael, Burton Lane, Jule Styne and other Hollywood grand dukes, but I have the distinction of having written a flop with him." By the mid-1930s, he tried his hand at singing and playing piano in nightclubs and began writing lyrics to music by Irving Actman. They contributed five songs to THE ILLUSTRATORS' SHOW, which opened January 22, 1936, and closed five performances later. It was a swift casualty on Broadway, but enough to land him a Hollywood contract, first with Universal, then Paramount, where he wrote his first film song, "The Moon of Manakoora," with Alfred Newman, for the Dorothy Lamour picture HURRICANE. He would go on to write lyrics for songs in over 60 films, including DESTRY RIDES AGAIN, NEPTUNE'S DAUGHTER, THANK YOUR LUCKY STARS, and Fred Astaire's LET'S DANCE.

War intervened, and Loesser was assigned to Special Services, providing lyrics for camp shows with such composers as Harold Rome and Alex North. Suddenly finding himself without a collaborator, Frank began his composing career with the war-time hit, "Praise the Lord and Pass the Ammunition." Later he told Jule Styne, "You boys showed me how it goes." He returned to Hollywood after the war, but struggling young producers Cy Feuer and Ernest Martin persuaded him to create a score for their projected Broadway musical of "Charley's Aunt," called WHERE'S CHARLEY? It opened October 11, 1948, and became Frank's first smash hit and Ray Bolger's greatest stage success. With a score that included "Once In Love with Amy," "My Darling, My Darling" and "Make a Miracle," WHERE'S CHARLEY? proved that Frank was more than just another pop tune writer from Hollywood. He followed that show with one of the great masterworks of American theater, GUYS AND DOLLS, which opened November 24, 1950, and quickly became a theatrical landmark, sweeping the Tony Awards for Best Musical, Best Book, Best Score, Best Actor, Best Supporting Actress, Best Director and Best Choreographer. His score was lush with hits, including "A Bushel and a Peck," "I've Never Been In Love Before," "Luck Be a Lady," "Fugue for Tinhorns," etc. Frank then took four years to write not only the score but also the book for his next show which he called an "extended musical comedy," THE MOST HAPPY FELLA. Although such opera-like works as PORGY AND BESS and STREET SCENE were unsuccessful initially, Frank's Napa Valley show with the hit songs "Standing on the Corner" and "Big D" opened May 3, 1956 and ran two years. It was the first show recorded in its entirety by Columbia Records. Reluctant to repeat himself, he decided on the country musical fable, GREENWILLOW, for his next project. In spite of

seven Tony nominations, it faltered and closed after 95 performances in 1960. Years later, Barbra Streisand made a hit song out of Greenwillow's "Never Will I Marry." On October 14, 1961, Frank bounced back with HOW TO SUCCEED IN BUSINESS WITHOUT REALLY TRYING, which won the Pulitzer Prize and seven Tony Awards, including Best Musical. It ran for four years on Broadway, with "I Believe in You" and "Brotherhood of Man" becoming enormous hits.

In the midst of all this stage work, Frank returned to Hollywood and created one of his best-loved scores for the film HANS CHRISTIAN ANDERSEN, which included "Wonderful Copenhagen," "Anywhere I Wander," "The Inch Worm," and "Thumbelina," nominated for an Academy Award. In 1974, Loesser's widow, Jo Sullivan, produced a long-running hit stage version called HANS ANDERSEN, starring Tommy Steele, at the Palladium in London.

The Loesser work pattern was directly related to the Loesser metabolism, which was extraordinary. He worked at a pace of unrelenting dynamism, rarely sleeping more than four hours a night. In the late 1940s, he formed his own music publishing company, Frank Music Corp., with the primary purpose of discovering and developing young composers and lyricists. He was instrumental in furthering the careers of the three most successful songwriters for the theater to emerge during the 1950s: Richard Adler, Jerry Ross and Meredith Willson. The company became a major force in American music publishing. Frank was married twice, first to actress Lynn Loesser, with whom he had two children, Susan and John, then to his MOST HAPPY FELLA leading lady, Jo Sullivan, who produced two daughters, Hannah and Emily. He died of lung cancer at the age of 59 on July 26, 1969, in his beloved New York City.

Frank Loesser forged only five Broadway musicals, but the Loesser impact continues to be seismic. A major production of THE MOST HAPPY FELLA appeared on Broadway in 1992 and the show was added to the New York City Opera's repertory. GUYS AND DOLLS won the 1992 Tony Award for Best Revival and is a smash hit on Broadway all over again. A new production of HOW TO SUCCEED IN BUSINESS is being readied for Broadway. DRG Records has released two important Loesser discs: "An Evening with Frank Loesser," a collection of recently discovered "demo" recordings Frank made for GUYS AND DOLLS, THE MOST HAPPY FELLA, and HOW TO SUCCEED IN BUSINESS WITHOUT REALLY TRYING, and "Loesser By Loesser," a compilation of both familiar and obscure songs performed by Jo Sullivan Loesser and her family. A biography written by Frank's daughter, Susan Loesser, called "A Most Remarkable Fella," has been published by Donald I. Fine, Inc. and the first complete collection of Loesser lyrics is scheduled for 1995.

Irving Actman and Frank Loesser, two aspiring song writers and an aspiring actress in Hollywood, mid-1930's.

Ray Bolger, George Abbott and Frank Loesser clowning around during the run of their smash Broadway hit **Where's Charley?**

Frank Loesser, Mary Martin and Jimmy McHugh during the filming of **Kiss The Boys Goodbye** *which Victor Schertzinger and Frank wrote for Mary. Frank and Jimmy wrote the great hit "Can't Get Out of this Mood" during this period.*

*Still from **Red, Hot and Blue***
Frank Loesser, June Havoc

Frank Loesser , Arthur Miller and Cy Feuer

*Frank Loesser and Kermit Bloomgarden outside the Shubert Theatre in Philadelphia during the pre-Broadway run of **The Most Happy Fella** in 1956.*

Frank Loesser and Irving Actman working together in New York

Publicity still of Frank Loesser from **Red, Hot and Blue**.

Singers had a strong effect on my father. He reviled them or he adored them or he married them. He pestered them, badgered them, coached them to tears. He once briefly walked off a show over a stubborn star. Fought a verbal duel over style with Frank Sinatra that left them lifelong enemies. Got so mad at one leading lady that he hauled off and hit her. Fell so madly in love with another soprano that he left my mother (also a singer) for her.

To some extent he must have viewed the singer as simply the instrument through which he spoke to his audience and, as such, the singer was not to interpret or show off or indulge in any quirks that might detract from the pure song pouring forth. My father expected singers to perform his songs clearly, meticulously, enunciating every word — with no deviation, no extra notes, no frivolous embellishments ("Singers love to vocalize beyond the sense of a lyric," he'd say. "They're always so sure you want to hear their goddamned tones!") — and he wanted it loud. If you couldn't project to the last row of the balcony without benefit of microphone, you had better not bother to audition for Frank Loesser.

I once sang for my father. It was a humiliating experience. I was thirteen. Among the many career choices I made frequently and feverishly in my teenage years, singing was — briefly — a favorite.

"Pop, I want to be a singer," I announced one day.

"Really! Do you really want to sing? Or do you just 'want to be a singer'? If you really want to sing, it has to be because you can't stand not singing. You'll never be any good if you want to be a singer just because you think it's a nice idea."

My heart had already begun to sink. I defensively asserted my deep love for the sound of my own voice in a glee club. I told him I really loved to sing (which, in fact, I did — sort of).

"Okay, why don't you come down to my office and audition for me tomorrow afternoon, after school," he said.

An audition! That was not what I had in mind. I had thought he'd suggest lessons, or give some mild encouragement. But my father had taken me all too seriously, and he challenged me the way he challenged everyone who came to him. "Show me your stuff. If you're good, I'll help you."

So, full of trepidation, the next day I stood and sang the Christmas carol I had selected while he accompanied me on the piano.

"Again. And louder," he said. And then, "Do it again in this higher key. And you're not projecting."

And so forth, for about two years, it seemed.

"I don't think you really have a gut love for this," he finally said. "And besides, you're nowhere near loud enough."

Even early in his career, when he was a struggling lyricist in Hollywood, my father raged and raved and carried on about how singers should sing. Eventually he found the phrase to crystallize his feeling. "Loud Is Good," he announced to the cast of THE MOST HAPPY FELLA. He had a sign made, and the maxim became Loesser dogma. It was audacious and outrageous and funny. It was just like him.

Excerpt courtesy of Susan Loesser from the recently published biography entitled
A MOST REMARKABLE FELLA.

Published by DONALD I. FINE, INC.
19 West 21st Street, New York, NY 10010
Distributed by PENGUIN, USA.

THE WORKS OF FRANK LOESSER

The following list of the published works of Frank Loesser is as complete and accurate as possible, given the state of information presently available. All songs written for a particular stage show are listed, whether or not they appeared in the final version. The same holds true for motion picture songs, except that songs used in a film <u>other</u> than that intended are listed under the title of the film in which they actually appeared.

It is amazing, in view of the extremely high quality of his subsequent composing, that most of Frank Loesser's early work was as lyricist, with his collaborators supplying the music. However, sometimes Mr. Loesser collaborated on the music, sometimes there were lyricist-collaborators, and sometimes the record is unclear. We have specified the nature of the collaboration where that information was available. In the case of the background film scores written with Irving Actman (who was later the music director of the stage production "Guys and Dolls"), presumably Mr. Actman and Mr. Loesser collaborated on the music.

1929
Melancholy Me *(music: Carl Rice)*

1930
Ticker Tape Talk *(music: Carl Rice)*

1931
In Love with a Memory of You
   (music: William H. Schuman)
Satan *(music: Carl Rice)*

1932
I'll See You in the Morning
   (music: Percy Wenrich)

1933
Hollywood Be Thy Name
   (vaudeville act; Jean Herbert)
Spaghetti
   (music: Otto Motzan; lyric: Billy Frisch)

1934
Doesn't That Mean Anything to You
   (music: Bob Emmerich)
Home Ties *(music: Charles Tobias,*
   Samuel Pokrass)
I Wish I Were Twins *(music: Joseph Meyer;*
   lyric: Edgar DeLange)
Junk Man *(music: Joseph Meyer)*
Now I Lay Me Down to Sin
Oh! What a Beautiful Baby You Turned
   Out to Be *(music: J. Fred Coots)*
The Old Oak Tree *(music: Joseph Meyer)*
ZIEGFELD FOLLIES OF 1934
   (stage show)
Goo Goo G'Da *(music: Ernest Breuer;*
   lyric: Billy Frisch, Raymond Leveen)

1935
I Just Came Back to Haunt You
   (Boogy Boogy Boogy Boo)
   (music: Bill Hueston, Bob Emmerich)
Sunday at Sundown *(Otto Motzan)*
The Traffic Was Terrific *(music:*
   Otto Motzan; lyric: Buddy Bernier)
POETIC GEMS *(motion picture:*
   15 original poems by Edgar A. Guest
   with descriptive songs; lyrics and music:
   Frank Loesser and Louis Herscher)
Back Seat Drivers
By a Silvery Stream
Don't Grow Any Older (My Little Boy Blue)
Down the Lane to Yesterday
Everybody's Ship Comes In (But Mine)
Get Under the Sun
Here's to the Builder
Indian Moon
Little Miss Mischief
A Real True Pal
The Snow Flakes
A Symphony in Green
Take Me Home to the Mountains

1936
A Tree in Tipperary *(music: Irving Actman)*
THE ILLUSTRATORS' SHOW
   (stage show; music: Irving Actman)
Bang, the Bell Rang
If You Didn't Love Me, Who Else Would
I Like to Go Strange Places
I'm You
Wild Trumpets and Crazy Piano (Got a
   Gal to Forget) *(music: Irving Actman)*

THE MAN I MARRY
   (motion picture; music: Irving Actman)
I Know I'm in Harlem
Old Homestead
POSTAL INSPECTOR
   (motion picture; music: Irving Actman)
Don't Let Me Love You
Hot Towel
Let's Have Bluebirds

1937
Dream Tonight *(music: Jackson Swales II)*
Here Comes Tomorrow (Gimme Another
   Kiss Goodnight) *(music: Irving Actman)*
BLOSSOMS ON BROADWAY *(motion*
   picture; music: Manning Sherwin)
Hold Your Hats, Here We Go Again
No Ring on Her Finger
You Can't Tell a Man by His Hat
Police Line Up
   (Grand Finale in Police Station)
THE DUCK HUNT *(background motion*
   picture score; Irving Actman)
A-Hunting We Will Go
The Decoy
Duck Antics
The Duck Fights
Duck Hunt Finale
In the Boat
A Run for It
Shooting
EVERYBODY SINGS *(background*
   motion picture score; Irving Actman)
Chasing
Chinese Serenade
Everybody Sings
Flight of the Birds

The 22-year old Frank Loesser in New York City.

March Song

Morning Serenade

Nobody But You

The Preacher's Sermon

Robber's Song

Run for Your Lives

The Scarecrow

Song of the Humming Birds

Song of the Sparrow

Three Black Crows

THE GOLFERS (THE GOLPHERS)

    (background motion picture score;

    Irving Actman)

Ball Dance

Can You Imagine

Folk Song

Golf Song

The Golphers Intermezzo

I Like You

Just for a Change

Meany Miny Moe

Nothing

Paraphrase

Scotch Air

Should I

Sleepy

THE HURRICANE (motion picture)

The Moon of Manakoora (music:

    Alfred Newman)

THE MYSTERIOUS CROSSING

    (motion picture; music: Irving Actman)

The Railroad That Ran Through Our Land

THREE SMART GIRLS (motion picture;

    music: Irving Actman; score not used)

Heart of Harlem

I Think You Have Got Something There

Life Is Peaches and Cream

Since When

You're My Heart

TURKEY DINNER (background motion

    picture score; music: Irving Actman)

Are You in Trouble

Do You Like Me?

Hot Bread

Hot Towel

Hot Turkey

Intermezzo

Just Like That

Tempest

Turkey Giblets

Turkey Trot

Turkey Dinner

VOGUES OF 1938 (motion picture)

Lovely One (music: Manning Sherwin)

YELLOWSTONE (motion picture)

Just Joggin' Along (music: Irving Actman)

1938_____

Let's Dream in the Moonlight

COCOANUT GROVE (motion picture;

    music: Burton Lane)

Says My Heart

Ten Easy Lessons (song based on a

    suggestion by Jack Rock)

COLLEGE SWING (motion picture)

Beans (music: Manning Sherwin)

College Swing (music: Hoagy Carmichael)

How'dja Like to Love Me

    (music: Burton Lane)

I Fall in Love with You Every Day

    (music: Manning Sherwin, Arthur Altman)

Moments Like This (music: Burton Lane)

The Old School Bell

    (music: Manning Sherwin)

Says My Heart (music: Manning Sherwin.

    Lyric used in "Cocoanut Grove")

Those Eyes You're Wearing

    (music: Burton Lane)

What a Rhumba Does to Romance

    (music: Manning Sherwin)

What Did Romeo Say to Juliet?

    (music: Burton Lane)

You're a Natural (music: Manning Sherwin)

FIGHT FOR YOUR LADY (motion picture)

Blame It on the Danube (music: Harry Akst)

FRESHMAN YEAR (motion picture)

Chasing You Around (music: Irving Actman)

GIVE ME A SAILOR

    (motion picture; music: Burton Lane)

Am I the Lucky One

Give Me a Sailor (music: Hoagy Carmichael)

I'm in Dreamland

I'm in the Pink

MEN WITH WINGS (motion picture)

Men with Wings (music: Hoagy Carmichael)

SING YOU SINNERS (motion picture)

Small Fry (music: Hoagy Carmichael)

A SONG IS BORN (motion picture)

Heart and Soul (music: Hoagy Carmichael)

SPAWN OF THE NORTH (motion picture;

    music: Burton Lane)

I Like Humped-Back Salmon

I Wish I Was the Willow

STOLEN HEAVEN (motion picture)

The Boys in the Band

    (music: Manning Sherwin)

THE TEXANS (motion picture)

I'll Come to the Wedding

    (music: traditional, "Buffalo Gals")

THANKS FOR THE MEMORY

    (motion picture)

Two Sleepy People

    (music: Hoagy Carmichael)

1939_____

Bubbles in the Wine (music: Bob Calame,

    Lawrence Welk; Welk theme song)

Fragrant Night (music: Louis Alter)

Here Comes the Night

    (music: Hilly Edelstein, Carl

    Hohengarten)

I Kinda Dream (music: Bernie Kane)

I'm All A-Tremble Over You

    (music: Ted Fiorito)

Old Fashioned Love (music: Fritz Miller)

$1,000 A TOUCHDOWN (motion picture)

Fight on for Madison (music: Victor Young)

BEAU GESTE (motion picture)

The Legionnaires' Song

    (music: Troy Sanders)

CAFE SOCIETY (motion picture)

Kiss Me with Your Eyes

    (music: Burton Lane)

Park Avenue Gimp (music: Leo Shuken)

DANCE WITH THE DEVIL

    (motion picture)

Your Kiss (music: Alfred Newman)

DESTRY RIDES AGAIN (motion picture;

    music: Frederick Hollander)

The Boys in the Backroom

Little Joe, the Wrangler

    (music based on traditional themes)

You've Got That Look (That Leaves Me Weak)

Frank Loesser in California – age 28.

THE GRACIE ALLEN MURDER CASE
 (motion picture)
A Flea Flew in My Flute
 (music: Phil Boutelje)
Snug as a Bug in a Rug
 (music: Matt Malneck)
HAWAIIAN NIGHTS
 (motion picture; music: Matt Malneck)
Hawaii Sang Me to Sleep
Hey, Good Lookin'
I Found My Love
Then I Wrote the Minuet in G (adapted
 from Ludwig Van Beethoven)
HERITAGE OF THE DESERT
 (motion picture)
Here's a Heart (music: Victor Young)
INVITATION TO HAPPINESS
 (motion picture)
Invitation to Happiness
 (music: Frederick Hollander)
ISLAND OF LOST MEN (motion picture)
Music on the Shore
 (music: Frederick Hollander)
THE LLANO KID
 (motion picture; music: Troy Sanders)
El Huapango
Starry Eyes (instrumental use only)
MAN ABOUT TOWN (motion picture;
 music: Frederick Hollander)
Fidgety Joe (music: Matt Malneck)
A Love Letter
Love with a Capital "You"
Man About Town
Petty Girl Routine
Strange Enchantment
That Sentimental Sandwich
SOME LIKE IT HOT (motion picture)
The Lady's in Love with You
 (music: Burton Lane)
Some Like It Hot
 (music: Gene Krupa, Remo Biondi)
Whodunit (music: Hoagy Carmichael)
ST. LOUIS BLUES
 (motion picture; music: Burton Lane)
Blue Nightfall
Don't Cry Little Cloud
I Go for That (Punkin's Dance)

 (music: Matt Malneck)
It's Grand
Junior
Oh, You Mississippi
She Was Wearing a Big Sombrero
The Song in My Heart Is a Rhumba
 (used in Latin American prints only)
THE STAR MAKER (motion picture)
Valse des Fleurs
 (music: Peter Illyich Tschaikowsky)
ZAZA (motion picture; music: Frederick
 Hollander)
Forget Me
He Died of Love
Hello, My Darling
I'm the Stupidest Girl in the Class
Street Song
Zaza

1940
By the By (music: "By" Woodbury)
ADVENTURES IN DIAMONDS
 (motion picture)
Whistler's Ditties (instrumental use only)
ALL WOMEN HAVE SECRETS
 (motion picture)
Rock-a-Bye Baby (music: Robert Burdette,
 Cano, Effie Canning; lyric:
 Frank Loesser, Johnny Cascales)
AT GOOD OLD SIWASH (motion picture)
Alpha Rho Song (music, traditional:
 "When Johnny Comes Marching
 Home"; lyric: C. Lambert)
Any Minute Now
Ode to Joy (Siwash Spring Song)
 (music: Beethoven's 9th Symphony)
Siwash Alma Mater
 (music: Beethoven's 9th Symphony)
We're All Here at Siwash (1)
 (music: Beethoven's 9th Symphony)
We're All Here at Siwash (2)
 (music: Johannes Brahms)
BUCK BENNY RIDES AGAIN
 (motion picture; music: Jimmy McHugh)
Drums in the Night
Music from Paradise
My Kind of Country
My! My!

Roses 'Round My Room
Say It (Over and Over Again)
That Friendly Feeling
THE FARMER'S DAUGHTER
 (motion picture)
Jungle Jingle
 (music: Frederick Hollander)
THE GREAT VICTOR HERBERT
 (motion picture) (lyrics written to
 pre-existing music by Victor Herbert)
Happy Days ("Punchinello"; lyric:
 Frank Loesser, Phil Boutelje)
Wonderful Dreams (or "Beautiful Dreams")
 ("Yesterthoughts")
You Are Beautiful ("Al Fresco"; lyric:
 Frank Loesser, Phil Boutelje)
DANCING FOR NICKELS AND DIMES
 (motion picture; music: Lionel Newman)
Dancing for Nickels and Dimes
This Is the Beginning of the End
MOON OVER BURMA (motion picture)
Mexican Magic (music: Harry Revel)
Moon Over Burma
 (music: Frederick Hollander)
A NIGHT AT EARL CARROLL'S (motion
 picture; music: Frederick Hollander)
I Wanna Make with the Happy Times
 (music: Gertrude Niesen)
I've Walked Through Wonderland
Li'l Boy Love
My Beautiful (music: Victor Young)
There Goes My Dream
NORTHWEST MOUNTED POLICE
 (motion picture)
Does the Moon Shine Through the Tall Pine?
 (music: Victor Young)
THE QUARTERBACK (motion picture)
Out with Your Chest (and Up with Your Chin)
 (music: Matt Malneck)
THE ROAD TO SINGAPORE
 (motion picture)
White Shadows on the Moon (White Mist
 of the Moon) (music: Victor Schertzinger)

Private Frank Loesser

THE WORKS OF FRANK LOESSER

SEVEN SINNERS *(motion picture;*
  music: Frederick Hollander)
I Fall Overboard
I've Been in Love Before
The Man's in the Navy
SEVENTEEN *(motion picture)*
Seventeen
TYPHOON *(motion picture)*
Palms of Paradise
  (music: Frederick Hollander)
YOUTH WILL BE SERVED
  (motion picture; music: Louis Alter)
Hot Catfish and Corn Dodgers
With a Banjo on My Knee
Youth Will Be Served

1941

ALOMA OF THE SOUTH SEAS *(motion*
  picture; music: Frederick Hollander)
Aloma of the South Seas
The Faraway Islands
The White Blossoms of Tah-Ni
ARIZONA SKETCHES *(motion picture)*
Prairieland Lullaby *(music: Victor Young)*
BIRTH OF THE BLUES *(motion picture)*
Memphis Blues *(music: W.C. Handy;*
  lyric: George A. Norton, revised by
  Frank Loesser)
CAUGHT IN THE DRAFT *(motion picture)*
Love Me As I Am *(music: Louis Alter)*
DANCING ON A DIME *(motion picture)*
Dancing on a Dime *(music: Burton Lane)*
Debutante Number One
  (music: Victor Young)
I Hear Music *(music: Burton Lane)*
Lovable Sort of Person
  (music: Victor Young)
Manana *(music: Burton Lane)*
Operatic Prelude to Show
  (music: Jule Styne)
GLAMOUR BOY *(motion picture;*
  music: Victor Schertzinger)
Love Is Such an Old Fashioned Thing
The Magic of Magnolias
HENRY FOR PRESIDENT *(motion picture)*
Johnny Jones *(music: Harry Barris)*
HOLD BACK THE DAWN *(motion picture)*
My Boy, My Boy *(music: Fred Spielman;*

  lyric: Jimmy Berg, Fred Jacobson)
KISS THE BOYS GOODBYE *(motion*
  picture; music: Victor Schertzinger)
Find Yourself a Melody
I'll Never Let a Day Pass By
Kiss the Boys Goodbye
Sand in My Shoes
(That's How I Got) My Start
There's No Forgetting You
We've Met Somewhere Before
LAS VEGAS NIGHTS *(motion picture)*
Dolores *(music: Louis Alter)*
I Gotta Ride *(music: Burton Lane)*
Mary, Mary, Quite Contrary
  (music: Burton Lane)
On Miami Shore *(music: Victor Young;*
  prologue lyric: Frank Loesser)
MANPOWER *(motion picture; music:*
  Frederick Hollander)
He Lied and I Listened
I'm in No Mood for Music Tonight
  (instrumental use only)
MR. BUG GOES TO TOWN *(motion*
  picture; music: Hoagy Carmichael)
Boy, Oh, Boy! *(music: Sammy Timberg)*
I'll Dance at Your Wedding (Honey Dear)
Katy-Did, Katy-Didn't
We're the Couple in the Castle
SAILORS ON LEAVE
  (motion picture; music: Jule Styne)
Sailor Routine
Sentimental Folks
Since You
When a Sailor Goes Ashore
SIS HOPKINS
  (motion picture; music: Jule Styne)
Cleopatra
Cracker Barrel County
Here We Are Studying History
If You're in Love
Look at You, Look at Me
  (music: Jule Styne, George Brown)
That Ain't Hay (That's the U.S.A.)
Well! Well!
THERE'S MAGIC IN MUSIC
  (motion picture)
Introduction

On Wings of Song
  (music: Felix Mendelssohn)
Toodles Imitation *(music: Phil Boutelje)*
You Tell Her, I Stutter
WORLD PREMIERE *(motion picture)*
Don't Cry Little Cloud *(music: Burton Lane)*

1942

Praise the Lord and Pass the Ammunition
BEYOND THE BLUE HORIZON
  (motion picture; music: Jule Styne)
Malay Love Song
Pagan Lullaby
THE FOREST RANGERS
  (motion picture)
Jingle Jangle Jingle (I Got Spurs That…)
  (music: Joseph J. Lilley)
Tall grows the Timber
  (music: Frederick Hollander)
PRIORITIES ON PARADE
  (motion picture; music: Jule Styne)
Here Comes Katrinka
I Said "No"
Johnny's Patter *(music: Troy Sanders;*
  lyric: Frank Loesser, Art Arthur)
Pay Day
You're in Love with Someone Else
  (But I'm in Love with You)
REAP THE WILD WIND *(motion picture)*
Sea Chanty *(music: Victor Young)*
SEVEN DAYS LEAVE *(motion picture;*
  music: Jimmy McHugh)
Baby
Can't Get Out of This Mood
I Get the Neck of the Chicken
Please, Won't You Leave My Girl Alone
Puerto Rico
Soft-Hearted
A Touch of Texas
You Speak My Language
SWEATER GIRL
  (motion picture; music: Jule Styne)
I Don't Want to Walk Without You
I Said "No"
Sweater Girl
What Gives Out Now?
THIS GUN FOR HIRE *(motion picture)*
I've Got You *(music: Jacques Press)*

Frank Loesser relaxing at the beach in the early 30's.

Now You See It, Now You Don't
   (music: Jacques Press)

I'm Amazed at You (music: Harold Spina)

TORTILLA FLAT
   (motion picture; music: Franz Waxman)

Ai Paisano (traditional: Franz Waxman,
   arranger)

Oh, How I Love a Wedding

TRUE TO THE ARMY
   (motion picture; music: Harold Spina)

In the Army

Jitterbug's Lullaby

Need I Speak

Ophelia

Spangles on My Tights

Swing in Line

Wacky for Khaki

We're Building Men
   (music: Joseph J. Lilley)

1943_____

Have I Stayed Away Too Long

The Sad Bombardier

ARMY SHOW (motion picture)

Hello, Mom (music: Eddie Dunstedter;
   lyric: Frank Loesser, Arthur V. Jones)

HAPPY-GO-LUCKY
   (motion picture; music: Jimmy McHugh)

The Fuddy Duddy Watchmaker

Happy-Go-Lucky

Jerry or Joe

Let's Get Lost

"Murder" He Says

Sing a Tropical Song

RIDING HIGH (motion picture)

Music from Paradise (music:
   Jimmy McHugh; instrumental use only)

THANK YOUR LUCKY STARS
   (motion picture; music: Arthur Schwartz)

The Dreamer

Good Night, Good Neighbor

How Sweet You Are

Ice Cold Katie

I'm Goin' North

I'm Ridin' for a Fall

Love Isn't Born (It's Made)

No You, No Me

Thank Your Lucky Stars

That's What You'll Jolly Well Get

They're Either Too Young or Too Old

We're Staying Home Tonight
   (My Baby and Me)

1944_____

My Gal's Working at Lockheed
   (Matt Dennis)

One Pip Wonder
   (Song of the Canadian Armored Corps)

Salute to the Army Service Forces

Stars on the Highway
   (music: Joseph Meyer)

ABOUT FACE (Armed Services revue)

Dog Face (music: Eddie Dunstedter)

First Class Private, Mary Brown

One Little W.A.C.
   (music: Eddie Dunstedter)

Why Do They Call a Private a Private?
   (music and lyric: Frank Loesser,
   Peter Lind Hayes)

AND THE ANGELS SING (motion picture)

Shake Hands with Your Neighbor
   (music: Victor Young)

CHRISTMAS HOLIDAY (motion picture)

Spring Will Be a Little Late This Year

DUFFY'S TAVERN
   (motion picture; radio series)

Leave Us Face It (We're in Love)
   (Abe Burrows)

HEAVENLY DAYS (motion picture)

Please Won't You Leave My Girl Alone
   (music: Jimmy McHugh)

HI, YANK (Armed Services revue;
   music: Eddie Dunstedter)

Classification Blues

General Orders

Little Red Rooftops

Most Important Job

My Gal and I

Yank, Yank, Yank

OK, USA (Armed Services revue)

When He Comes Home

SEE HERE, PRIVATE HARGROVE
   (motion picture)

In My Arms (music: Ted Grouya)

THE SHINING FUTURE (motion picture)

The Road to Victory

SKIRTS (Armed Services revue)

Skirts

TORNADO (motion picture)

There Goes My Dream
   (music: Frederick Hollander)

THE W.A.C. MUSICAL
   (Armed Services revue)

The W.A.C. Hymn

1945_____

Kiss at Midnight
   (music and lyric: Frank Loesser,
   Irving Actman, Dailey Paskman)

Rodger Young

Wave to Me, My Lady (music and lyric:
   Frank Loesser, William Stein)

BEHIND CITY LIGHTS (motion picture)

If You're in Love (music: Jule Styne)

1946_____

THE DAY BEFORE SPRING
   (unproduced motion picture; music:
   Johnny Green)

Bing Bang

Ibbedy Bibbedy Sibbedy Sab

It's Time for the Love Scene

My Sentimental Nature

Opening

Statue Song (incomplete)

Who Could Forget You

You're So Reliable

LADY CALLED LOU (motion picture)

Goldie Goes with the Mine

Misty Eyed (music: Matt Malneck)

What Kind of Fool

STRANGE TRIANGLE (motion picture)

Your Kiss (music: Alfred Newman)

1947_____

Bloop! Bleep!

Keep Your Eye on the Sky

Night Blooming Jasmine
   (music: Matt Malneck)

Silver Bells (music: Joseph J. Lilley)

A Tune for Humming

What Are You Doing New Year's Eve?

A MIRACLE CAN HAPPEN (motion picture)

The Queen of the Hollywood Islands

THE WORKS OF FRANK LOESSER

THE PERILS OF PAULINE
(motion picture)

I Wish I Didn't Love You So
(Academy Award nomination)

Poppa, Don't Preach to Me

Rumble, Rumble, Rumble

The Sewing Machine

VARIETY GIRL (motion picture)

The Fireman's Ball

The French Get So Excited

Grauman's Chinese Sequence

He Can Waltz

Impossible Things

I Must Have Been Madly In Love

I Want My Money Back

Tallahassee

The Tunnel of Love

Your Heart Calling Mine

1948_____

Anna (music: Victor Schertzinger)

Down the Stairs, Out the Door
(Went My Baby)

The Feathery Feelin'

The Last Thing I Want Is Your Pity

LADY FROM LARIAT LOOP (motion picture)

Batten Down Her Hatches

Pindy-Fendy (Indian chant)

LET'S DANCE (motion picture)

Can't Stop Talking (About Him)

The Hyacinth

I'll Always Love You

Jack and the Beanstalk

The Ming Toy Noodle

Oh, Them Dudes (production number)

The Tunnel of Love

Why Fight the Feeling

NEPTUNE'S DAUGHTER (motion picture)

Baby, It's Cold Outside
(Academy Award winner)

I Love Those Men

I Want My Money Back

My Heart Beats Faster

Neptune's Daughter

WHERE'S CHARLEY? (stage show;
opened October 11, 1948;
motion picture 1953)

The Argument

At the Red Rose Cotillion

The Bee

Better Get Out of Here

Don't Introduce Me to that Angel

The Gossips

Lovelier Than Ever

Make a Miracle

My Darling, My Darling

The New Ashmolean Marching Society
and Students Conservatory Band

Once in Love with Amy

Pernambuco

Saunter Away

Serenade with Asides

The Train That Brought You to Town

Where's Charley?

The Woman in His Room

The Years Before Us

Your Own College Band

1949_____

RED, HOT AND BLUE (motion picture)

Hamlet

I Wake Up in the Morning Feeling Fine

Now That I Need You (Where Are You...)

That's Loyalty

ROSEANNA McCOY (motion picture)

Roseanna

1950_____

Hoop-Dee-Doo (music: Milton Delugg)

GUYS AND DOLLS (stage show; opened
November 24, 1950)

Adelaide's Lament

A Bushel and a Peck

Follow the Fold

Fugue for Tinhorns

Getting Dressed

Guys and Dolls

If I Were a Bell

I'll Know

It Feels Like Forever

I've Never Been in Love Before

Luck Be a Lady

Marry the Man Today

More I Cannot Wish You

My Time of Day

The Oldest Established

Shango

Sit Down You're Rockin' the Boat

Sue Me

Take Back Your Mink

Traveling Light

1951_____

Three Cornered Tune
(lyric written to "Fugue for Tinhorns"
from GUYS AND DOLLS)

THE COLLEGE BOWL (motion picture)

Meet Me at the College Bowl

1952_____

Makes Me Feel Good All Over

Stone Walls

HANS CHRISTIAN ANDERSEN
(motion picture)

Anywhere I Wander

Dream Fantasy

I'm Hans Christian Andersen

The Inch Worm

The King's New Clothes

Metronome Fantasy

No Two People

Royal Danish

The Shoe Song

Street Voices

Thumbelina (Academy Award nomination)

The Ugly Duckling

Wedding Fantasy

Wonderful Copenhagen

MY SON JOHN (motion picture)

Girls School Alma Mater
(music: Franz Waxman)

1953_____

All Is Forgiven (All Is Forgotten)

Benny to Helen to Chance
(music: Milton Delugg)

Crying Polka (music: Milton Delugg)

Just Another Polka (music: Milton Delugg)

No Swallerin' Place (June Carter)

1954_____

Such a Sudden Spring
(music: Irving Actman)

Frank's favorite picture of himself, taken by Sam Shaw.

THE WORKS OF FRANK LOESSER

Thunder and Lightning

To Marry

To Your Health

Truly Loved

Turkish Delight

What Is Life

*1969*_____

SENOR DISCRETION

    (unproduced stage show)

Campaneros

Heaven Smiles on Tepancingo

I Cannot Let You Go

I Got to Have a Somebody

I Love Him

Mexico City

Padre, I Have Sinned

Pan Pan Pan

Pancito, She would Call Me

Papa, Come home

The Paseo

To See Her

The Wisdom of the Heart

World Peace

You Understand Me

*1974*_____

Asking for Trouble

That Was My Love I Gave You

HANS ANDERSEN *(stage show;*

    opened London, December 17, 1974)

Jenny Kissed Me *(new lyric to "Don't*

    Introduce Me To That Angel" from

    WHERE'S CHARLEY?; lyric:

    Marvin Laird)

ADELAIDE

(From The Motion Picture "GUYS AND DOLLS")

By FRANK LOESSER

27

Refrain *(with a sentimental lilt)*

ADELAIDE'S LAMENT
(From "GUYS AND DOLLS")

By FRANK LOESSER

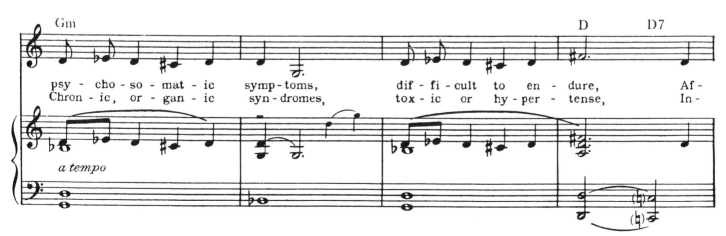

ANYWHERE I WANDER

(From The Motion Picture "HANS CHRISTIAN ANDERSEN")

By FRANK LOESSER

BABY, IT'S COLD OUTSIDE
(From The Motion Picture "NEPTUNE'S DAUGHTER")

Words and Music by
FRANK LOESSER

38

BROTHERHOOD OF MAN
(From "HOW TO SUCCEED IN BUSINESS WITHOUT REALLY TRYING")

Handclapping Spiritual Feel

By FRANK LOESSER

A BUSHEL AND A PECK
(From "GUYS AND DOLLS")

By FRANK LOESSER

Light Bounce Tempo

BIG D
(From "THE MOST HAPPY FELLA")

By FRANK LOESSER

Brightly

You're from Big D_____ I can guess_____ by the way you drawl___ and the way you dress___ You're from Big D, My, oh yes.___

FUGUE FOR TINHORNS

(From "GUYS AND DOLLS")

By FRANK LOESSER

48

CAN'T GET OUT OF THIS MOOD
(From The Motion Picture "SEVEN DAYS LEAVE")

By FRANK LOESSER
and JIMMY McHUGH

54

GUYS AND DOLLS
(From "GUYS AND DOLLS")

By FRANK LOESSER

HEART AND SOUL
(From The Paramount Short Subject "A SONG IS BORN")

Words by FRANK LOESSER
Music by HOAGY CARMICHAEL

I BELIEVE IN YOU
(From "HOW TO SUCCEED IN BUSINESS WITHOUT REALLY TRYING")

By FRANK LOESSER

63

64

65

I DON'T WANT TO
WALK WITHOUT YOU

(From The Paramount Picture "SWEATER GIRL")

Words by FRANK LOESSER
Music by JULE STYNE

71

I HEAR MUSIC
(From The Paramount Picture "DANCING ON A DIME")

Lyrics by FRANK LOESSER
Music by BURTON LANE

Verse

Not that I'm a Pun-chi-nel - lo. Just an op-ti-mis-tic fel - low with a lot of ver-y mel-low mu-sic in my soul.— Not that I'm a Pol-ly-an - na, shout-in' out a loud ho-san - na. It's my sing-ing heart I can't con-trol._____

Refrain

74

I WISH I DIDN'T LOVE YOU SO

(From The Paramount Picture "THE PERILS OF PAULINE")

By FRANK LOESSER

I'LL KNOW
(From "GUYS AND DOLLS")

By FRANK LOESSER

I'M HANS CHRISTIAN ANDERSEN

(From The Motion Picture "HANS CHRISTIAN ANDERSEN")

By FRANK LOESSER

1. I'M HANS CHRIS-TIAN AN - DER-SEN, I've man-y a tale to tell   And
HANS CHRIS-TIAN AN - DER-SEN, I bring you a fa - ble   rare   There
HANS CHRIS-TIAN AN - DER-SEN, My pen's like a bab-bling brook   Per-

though I'm a cob - bler,   I'd   say   I tell them rath - er   well   I'll
once was a ta - ble,   who said   "Oh how I'd love a   chair"   And
mit   me to show you,   Dear sir,   my ver - y la - test   book   Now

82

I'VE NEVER BEEN IN LOVE BEFORE

(From "GUYS AND DOLLS")

By FRANK LOESSER

IF I WERE A BELL

(From "GUYS AND DOLLS")

By FRANK LOESSER

Medium Bounce

IN YOUR EYES

(From "PLEASURES AND PALACES")

By FRANK LOESSER

THE INCH WORM

(From The Motion Picture "HANS CHRISTIAN ANDERSEN")

By FRANK LOESSER

Refrain

JOEY, JOEY, JOEY
(From "THE MOST HAPPY FELLA")

By FRANK LOESSER

JUNK MAN

Lyric by FRANK LOESSER
Music by JOSEPH MEYER

8va

THE LADY'S IN LOVE WITH YOU

(From The Paramount Picture "SOME LIKE IT HOT")

Lyric by FRANK LOESSER
Music by BURTON LANE

LET'S GET LOST

(From The Paramount Picture "HAPPY GO LUCKY")

By FRANK LOESSER
and JIMMY McHUGH

LOVE ISN'T BORN, IT'S MADE

(From The Motion Picture "THANK YOUR LUCKY STARS")

Words by FRANK LOESSER
Music by ARTHUR SCHWARTZ

Oh my pre - cious young dove if you're dream - ing of love, you've

got to join in the chase your - self,__ and here's my sto - ry, so brace your - self:__

LOVELIER THAN EVER

(From "WHERE'S CHARLEY?")

By FRANK LOESSER

116

LUCK BE A LADY
(From "GUYS AND DOLLS")

By FRANK LOESSER

THE MOON OF MANAKOORA
(From The Motion Picture "THE HURRICANE")

Lyric by FRANK LOESSER
Music by ALFRED NEWMAN

124

"MURDER," HE SAYS
(From The Paramount Picture "HAPPY GO LUCKY")

Words by FRANK LOESSER
Music by JIMMY McHUGH

* *Chord Names For Guitar*

MORE I CANNOT WISH YOU

(From "GUYS AND DOLLS")

By FRANK LOESSER

THE MUSIC OF HOME
(From "GREENWILLOW")

By FRANK LOESSER

136

MY HEART IS SO FULL OF YOU

(From "THE MOST HAPPY FELLA")

By FRANK LOESSER

140

MY DARLING, MY DARLING
(From "WHERE'S CHARLEY?")

By FRANK LOESSER

Moderately

MY TIME OF DAY
(From "GUYS AND DOLLS")

By FRANK LOESSER

NEVER WILL I MARRY

(From "GREENWILLOW")

By FRANK LOESSER

Bet - ter look her look - ing some oth - er way, _____

For my kiss can be no ev - er-more prom - ise, _____

But a fan - cy danc - y fid - dle and free. _____

THE NEW ASHMOLEAN MARCHING SOCIETY AND STUDENTS CONSERVATORY BAND

(From "WHERE'S CHARLEY?")

By FRANK LOESSER

155

156

NO TWO PEOPLE

(From The Motion Picture "HANS CHRISTIAN ANDERSEN")

By FRANK LOESSER

158

NOW THAT I NEED YOU
(WHERE ARE YOU?)
(From The Paramount Picture "RED, HOT AND BLUE!")

By FRANK LOESSER

THE OLDEST ESTABLISHED

(From "GUYS AND DOLLS")

By FRANK LOESSER

Bright tempo

ON A SLOW BOAT TO CHINA

Words and Music by
FRANK LOESSER

Slowly, with a beat

ONCE IN LOVE WITH AMY

(From "WHERE'S CHARLEY?")

By FRANK LOESSER

PET ME, POPPA

(From The Motion Picture "GUYS AND DOLLS")

By FRANK LOESSER

Refrain *(with a beat)*

180

POPPA, DON'T PREACH TO ME

(From The Paramount Picture "THE PERILS OF PAULINE")

Words and Music by
FRANK LOESSER

Nat-'ral - ly I read what she wrote,

This is what she said, and I quote:

Refrain

I came to Par - is to buy me a gown,— To
I danced in Par - is last night with Pi - erre,— That
I'm here in Par - is since ear - ly in May,— My

Par - is, to Par - is, And oh, what a town!— The
"X" marks my room, but I'm nev - er up there,— I
gown got all worn out but I'm still o - kay,— I'm

184

185

ROSEANNA
(From The Motion Picture "ROSEANNA McCOY")

By FRANK LOESSER

187

RUMBLE, RUMBLE, RUMBLE

(From The Paramount Picture "THE PERILS OF PAULINE")

Words and Music by
FRANK LOESSER

191

SAND IN MY SHOES

(From The Paramount Picture "KISS THE BOYS GOODBYE")

By FRANK LOESSER
and VICTOR SCHERTZINGER

*Symbols for Guitar

SAY IT
(OVER AND OVER AGAIN)
(From The Paramount Picture "BUCK BENNY RIDES AGAIN")

Words by FRANK LOESSER
Music by JIMMY McHUGH

200

A SECRETARY IS NOT A TOY

(From "HOW TO SUCCEED IN BUSINESS WITHOUT REALLY TRYING")

By FRANK LOESSER

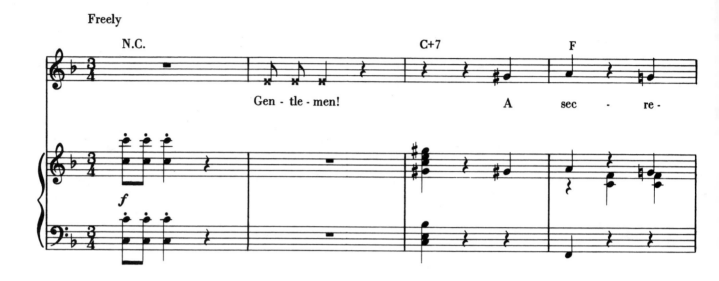

SIT DOWN YOU'RE ROCKIN' THE BOAT

(From "GUYS AND DOLLS")

By FRANK LOESSER

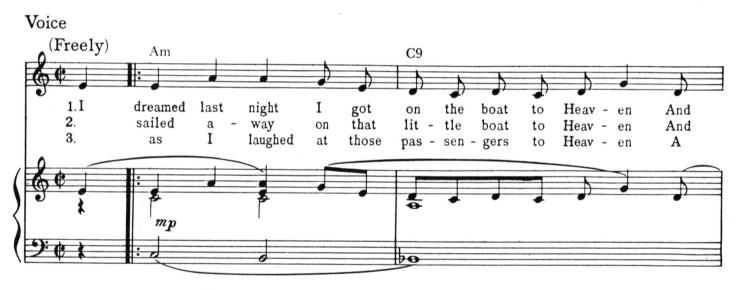

1.I dreamed last night I got on the boat to Heav - en And
2. sailed a - way on that lit - tle boat to Heav - en And
3. as I laughed at those pas - sen - gers to Heav - en A

by some chance I had brought my dice a - long, And
by some chance found a bot - tle in my fist, And
great big wave came and washed me ov - er - board, And

Chorus with a beat

212

SOMEBODY, SOMEWHERE

(From "THE MOST HAPPY FELLA")

By FRANK LOESSER

SMALL FRY
(From The Paramount Picture "SING, YOU SINNERS")

Words by FRANK LOESSER
Music by HOAGY CARMICHAEL

SPRING WILL BE A LITTLE LATE THIS YEAR

(From The Motion Picture "CHRISTMAS HOLIDAY")

By FRANK LOESSER

222

STANDING ON THE CORNER
(From "THE MOST HAPPY FELLA")

By FRANK LOESSER

SUE ME

(From "GUYS AND DOLLS")

By FRANK LOESSER

SUMMERTIME LOVE

(From "GREENWILLOW")

By FRANK LOESSER

cool in the nip of Sep - tem - ber. _____ Now they

point to the skies, do the old and the wise, _____ And they

speak of a chill in the air. And they wink while they're nudg - ing me

In tempo (bright)

o - ver to the pret - ty lit - tle la - dies in the square. _____

235

TALLAHASSEE
(From The Paramount Picture "VARIETY GIRL")

By FRANK LOESSER

THUMBELINA

(From The Motion Picture "HANS CHRISTIAN ANDERSEN")

By FRANK LOESSER

242

THEY'RE EITHER TOO YOUNG OR TOO OLD
(From The Motion Picture "THANK YOUR LUCKY STARS")

Words by FRANK LOESSER
Music by ARTHUR SCHWARTZ

Slowly, with a beat

A TUNE FOR HUMMING

By FRANK LOESSER

TWO SLEEPY PEOPLE

(From The Paramount Picture "THANKS FOR THE MEMORY")

Words by FRANK LOESSER
Music by HOAGY CARMICHAEL

TRAVELING LIGHT
(From "GUYS AND DOLLS")

By FRANK LOESSE

Cm
G7
G7♯5
car - ry, Though your prop - o - si - tion's a
Cm
C7
Fm
beaut. And I'm damned if your sis - ter I'll
C
B♭dim
Am7
D7
mar - ry, Guess I left my heart in my
A♭7♭5
G7
C
Cm7
E♭/G
D♭/G
E♭/G
oth - er suit. And I'm trav - el - ing light, No one's

WARM ALL OVER

(From "THE MOST HAPPY FELLA")

By FRANK LOESSER

THE UGLY DUCKLING
(From The Motion Picture "HANS CHRISTIAN ANDERSEN")

By FRANK LOESSER

WHAT ARE YOU DOING NEW YEAR'S EVE?

Words and Music
FRANK LOESSE[R]

Slowly and sentimentally

When the bells all ring, _____ and the horns all blow, _____ And th[e]

cou-ples we know _____ are fond-ly kiss-ing, _____ Will I

be with you, _____ or will I be a-mong the miss-ing? _____

A WOMAN IN LOVE

(From The Motion Picture "GUYS AND DOLLS")

By FRANK LOESSER

WONDERFUL COPENHAGEN

(From The Motion Picture "HANS CHRISTIAN ANDERSEN")

By FRANK LOESSER